I0157231

The principal objective of THE MATHESON TRUST is to promote the study of comparative religion from the point of view of the underlying harmony of the great religious and philosophical traditions of the world. This objective is being pursued through such means as audio-visual media, the support and sponsorship of lecture series and conferences, the creation of a website, collaboration with film production companies and publishing companies as well as the Trust's own series of publications.

The Matheson Monographs cover a wide range of themes within the field of comparative religion: scriptural exegesis in different religious traditions; the modalities of spiritual and contemplative life; in-depth mystical studies of particular religious traditions; broad comparative analyses taking in a series of religious forms; studies of traditional arts, crafts and cosmological science; and contemporary scholarly expositions of religious philosophy and metaphysics. The monographs also comprise translations of both classical and contemporary texts, as well as transcriptions of lectures by, and interviews with, spiritual and scholarly authorities from different religious and philosophical traditions.

IN THAT LUMINOUS DARKNESS

Vicente Pascual Rodrigo in 2005

IN THAT LUMINOUS DARKNESS

Selected Poems by
Vicente Pascual Rodrigo

Spanish-English Edition

Translated from the Spanish by

William Wroth and
Susana Marín

THE MATHESON TRUST
For the Study of Comparative Religion

Spanish text © Ana Marquina, 2020
English translation © Deborah Wroth, 2020

This first edition published by

The Matheson Trust
PO Box 336
56 Gloucester Road
London SW7 4UB, UK

www.themathesontrust.org

ISBN: 978 1 908092 19 9

*All rights reserved. No part of this publication
may be reproduced, stored in a retrieval system,
or transmitted in any form or by any means, electronic,
mechanical, photocopying, recording, or otherwise,
without the prior written permission of the Publisher.*

British Library Cataloguing-in-Publication Data.
A catalogue record for this book is
available from the British Library.

Typeset by the publishers in Baskerville 10 Pro.

Cover image: Painting by Vicente Pascual Rodrigo
courtesy of Ana Marquina
Cover design by Susana Marín.

CONTENTS

INTRODUCTION

In this book we want to introduce the reader to the work of a Spanish poet who, although highly regarded in his native land, is little known in the English-speaking world. At a time when much poetry lacks meaning or means of access, Vicente Pascual Rodrigo's work is refreshing in its contrast to more superficial verse and refreshing in the sense of revitalizing—a refreshment to the spirit and the soul. In Pascual's work one may find a teaching which contemplates the most elemental questions of life, love, and death—yet it is neither didactic nor sectarian. His verse does not give final answers to these questions—for who can presume to do so?—but vividly presents them to the reader. Through his evocative and musical language he communicates these timeless human issues which concern all of us regardless of language or culture.

Vicente Pascual Rodrigo was born in 1955 in Zaragoza, Spain. He began his career as an artist, studying at the Escuela de Artes of Zaragoza and at the Escuela de Bellas Artes of Barcelona. From 1970 to 1988, he worked and exhibited his work with his brother Ángel Pascual Rodrigo in the two-man collective, *La Hermandad Pictórica*. After a journey through Afghanistan, Pakistan, and India in 1974-75, Pascual established his own studio first in Aragón (1975) and then in Majorca (1981). In 1992, he moved to the United States and lived there until 2003 when he moved back to Spain. He died in Zaragoza in 2008. His work is held in many public and private collections in both Spain and the United States.[1]

---

[1] Pascual's work is in numerous international collections including The Hispanic Society of America in New York; Calcografía Nacional in Madrid; George Washington University, Washington DC; Indiana University Art Museum; Museu d'Art Modern i Contemporani, Palma de Mallorca; Museo Pablo Serrano, Zaragoza; and La Caixa, Barcelona.

During the last decade of his life he began writing poetry and published several volumes in Spain. In 2006 his book of poems and paintings, *Las 100 vistas del Monte Interior: En Recuerdo de los Antiguos Locos*, was published by the Government of Aragón, in collaboration with Olifante Ediciones de Poesía. It was followed in 2007 by *A la Vida, a la Muerte y a mi Bienamada: Cancioncillas y cancionejas* (Papeles de Trasmoz, Olifante Ediciones de Poesía). A third book, *De la Nada Nada Viene*, was published in 2010 (Colección Veruela Poesía de Olifante). In 2009 a major retrospective exhibition of his paintings was mounted in Zaragoza, accompanied by a catalogue raisonné of 240 pages.[2] This catalogue includes, in addition to scholarly essays on his work, a selection of 45 of his poems.

His book *A la Vida, a la Muerte y mi Bienamada* has a prologue by the renowned Spanish poet José Corredor-Matheos (winner of the Premio Nacional de Poesía in 2005), and was edited by another leading Spanish poet, Ángel Guinda. Concerning Pascual, Guinda suggests that

> Vicente Pascual, in addition to being an ineffable painter, has always been a worthy and exemplary secret poet. His paintings enclose an atmosphere of profound and transcendent lyricism. The secret of his poetry was only revealed when his precarious physical health obliged him to paint with words, leaving us poems of exquisite simplicity, depth and spirituality.[3]

The power and beauty of his verse places Pascual within the great

---

[2] *Vicente Pascual 1989/2008: Opusculum*. Zaragoza: Palacio de Sástago, Diputación Provincial de Zaragoza, 2009. Other recent exhibitions in Spain include: 'Vicente Pascual: Imago Silenti', Galería Edurne, Madrid, 2007; 'No Hay Vino Si No Hay Agua', Centro Cultural Mariano Mesonada, Utebo, Zaragoza, 2008; and 'Vicente Pascual: Pinturas y Dibujos, 2000–2008', Museo Salvador Victoria, Rubielos de Mora, Teruel, Aragon, 2011.

[3] Ángel Guinda, 'Vicente Pascual, poeta secreto' in *Vicente Pascual 1989/2008: Opusculum*, 195: 'Vicente Pascual, además de pintor inefable, ha sido siempre un poeta secreto, digno y ejemplar. Su obra plástica encierra una atmósfera de lirismo profundo, trascendente. El secretismo de su poesía sólo se vio roto cuando la precariedad física, que no intelectual, le obligó a pintar con la palabra, dejándonos poemas de una sencillez, hondura y espiritualidad exquisitas.'

tradition of Spanish poetry. José Corredor-Matheos, in his intro-
duction to *A la Vida, a la Muerte y mi Bienamada*, favorably compares
his verse to that of the sixteenth-century Carmelite friar, San Juan
de la Cruz:

> 'The vision of the visible world, and, if I may say so, of the
> invisible—which in poetry must always be made visible in one
> way or another—and the tremor and glow of his verse have
> the flavor of the poetry of San Juan de la Cruz: 'Like that doe
> among the crags. / Such is/ the lullaby of my beloved.' But we
> know that the great mystic poet, one of the most sublime of
> world literature, is part of a long tradition of understanding
> poetry as a manifestation of a sacred feeling, relating, on some
> level, with Sufism....'

One can also see influences from masters of the past century, such
as the sparing lyrics of Juan Ramón Jiménez, or Antonio Machado's
powerful and riveting verse. Machado was well aware that the es-
sence of true poetry is 'the deep pulse of the spirit':

> I thought that the substance of poetry does not lie in the sound
> value of the word, nor in its color, nor in the metric line, nor in
> the complex of sensations, but in the deep pulse of the spirit;
> and this deep pulse is what the soul contributes ... with its own
> voice, in a courageous answer to the touch of the world.[4]

In Pascual's work, as Corredor-Matheos suggests, there is a quality
that transcends nationality, a spiritual directness that goes to the
heart of the matter. Pascual found sustenance for both his visual
work and his poetry in several religious and aesthetic traditions.
In the introduction (which he titled 'Obligatory Warning') to his
first book, *Las 100 vistas del Monte Interior*, he wrote in typically self-

---

[4] Antonio Machado, *Soledades, Galerías y Otros Poemas*, Madrid, 1917. 'Pensaba
yo que el elemento poético no era la palabra por su valor fónico, ni el color,
ni la línea, ni un complejo de sensaciones, sino una honda palpitación del es-
píritu, lo que pone el alma... con voz propia, en respuesta animada al contacto
del mundo.'

deprecating manner about the variety of influences which inform his work:

> I have copied the Pre-Socratics, the Neo-Platonists and the songs of the Native Americans.... I have imitated the Taoists, the Hindus; I have drawn upon those, like Rumi and Nizāmī, who understood the coherent beauty of the formulations of Sufism. I have imitated the Spanish Carmelites, the Fideli d'Amore, the medieval Rhenish mystics....

The range of sources he enumerates here suggests the depth of his devotion to the inner search for understanding, for knowledge, for a path that would draw closer to God. His spiritual search began in earnest in the early 1970s when he lived among traditional peoples in India, Pakistan and Afghanistan whence he embarked on a life-long devotion to study of the spiritual traditions enumerated in his statement above: Greek philosophy and Neo-Platonism, Taoism, Hinduism, Sufism and medieval and later Christian mysticism.

He was equally inspired by the oral and material expressions of indigenous peoples. In a preface to the catalogue for a 1994 exhibition of his paintings, he wrote of his admiration for the Tuaregs of Africa, the Native Americans, and the Mongolians, whose artistic expressions have

> shaped my work for the last few years ... what arouses my interest is not the customs of any particular ethnic group, but the universal element which they have in common. This is what produces an echo in my being and rebounds in a form of expression which is shaped by my artistic development, a European education, by a set of experiences and memories. As Basho might have said: 'I do not follow the ancient nomads, I am looking for what they were searching for.'[5]

Clearly he was searching for and trying to express in his work the 'universal element' which all these traditions, appearing so varied on the surface, share in common.

---

[5] Essay for his *Nómadas* exhibition catalogue. Madrid: Galería Edurne, 1994.

His painting during a career of more than thirty years went through a slow process of change as he gradually shed reliance on the exterior world of objects and landscapes, simplifying his vision, yet at the same time maintaining a consummate mastery of forms and colors at their most elemental levels. In the 1994 preface cited above he wrote: 'my paintings have been stripped of the veil, the landscape's forms which covered them.'

This process of essentialization also took place in his poetry. It is the verbal expression of the changes taking place within himself. The gradual deepening of his understanding of the nature of reality and the place of human beings in this world found expression in his verse. For Pascual poetry could not be a mental game or shallow self-revealing: his words hit home because they are real.

Meanings such as those conveyed in Pascual's verse raise questions unanswerable by rational thought—otherwise poetry would not differ in any significant way from prose discourse. Poetry is heightened language that embodies levels of significance that take the reader or listener beyond the mundane world. Sound is the form and the means by which meaning is conveyed: the music of the poem is redolent with meanings. The music of the poem evokes feelings in the heart of the reader, feelings that in turn evoke meanings because they come as words. To reach the heart, such music must come from the heart. Pascual summed it up thus: '*Ab Intra Ad Intra.*' The translator and scholar Bill Porter (Red Pine) noted regarding Chinese poetry: 'The original meaning of the Chinese word for poetry (*shih*) was "words from the heart."'[6]

Words from the heart of the poet to the heart of the reader. In Pascual's work, heart must be understood in a deeper sense than merely the place of the emotions. The heart in many religious traditions is the center of the being and as such is the locus where

---

[6] Bill Porter, *Zen Baggage*, Berkeley: Counterpoint, 2009, p. 26. Bill Porter has further elaborated on the act of creation: 'Poetry is not simply "words from the heart." A poet doesn't make a poem so much as discover a poem.... In poetry, we go beyond ourselves to the heart of the universe, where we might be moved by something as small as a grain of sand or as great as the Ganges.' ('Dancing with the Dead: Language, Poetry, and the Art of Translation' in *Cipher Journal* http://www.cipherjournal.com/html/red_pine.html).

understanding takes place. Understanding, knowledge in a full sense, must of course include the emotions. 'Know thyself' means to know fully one's own heart. For the poet words from the heart bring forth something deeper than surface concerns or the superficial ego, and thus they have a transformative power. Vicente Pascual wrote the following concerning the act of painting, which also applies to his poetry:

> Art makes sense precisely because man has the need to free himself from the ego which restrains him and the world which fragments him. Through creation, he exteriorizes what he loves or knows in order to interiorize and assimilate it through a process of objectivation.[7]

Through the medium of words Pascual provides the means to escape from the tyranny of words, of language itself. In our everyday world words tend to have univocal meanings. They have precision, yes, but that very quality can limit us to the mundane, the practical, the socially agreed-upon meaning. To escape the tyranny of words through multi-vocal meanings is for Pascual a means to approach closer to the Divine, to the Nameless that is beyond names, thus beyond words.

Here Pascual frequently touches on one of the exigencies of the path of early Christian and other mystics who followed the via negativa: that which can be named, or defined by a name, is not the ultimate reality. The Dionysian texts, for instance, state: 'And so it is that as Cause of all and as transcending all, he is rightly nameless and yet has the names of everything that is.'[8] This approach is found in other religions, for instance, the method called 'neti, neti' (not this, not this) in Hinduism.

Pascual's work is clearly inspired by the great spiritual traditions in many religions: Christianity, Judaism, Islam, Buddhism, American Indian and others. Immersion in these traditions and understanding of what they share in common played a necessary

---

[7] *Nómadas* exhibition catalogue.

[8] *Pseudo-Dionysius: The Complete Works*. Colm Luibheid and Paul Rorem, ed. and trans., New York : Paulist Press, 1987, 56 ('The Divine Names,' 596D)

role in his maturation. He came to understand from them that the purpose of life was not to search for material gain or worldly accomplishments, but to embark upon a quest to find deeper understanding of what it means to be human. He saw both his painting and poetry not merely as art forms, but as practices having a larger meaning, a way of understanding the meaning of life. Thus for him these exterior expressions have primarily an interior purpose. They add a form and a leavening to that inner alchemy so essential in the search for self-knowledge.

It may also lead to addressing the unknown within the reader, the unrealized potential of one's own soul which contains the whole universe: 'The universe within us;/and we a drop of dew.'[9] Here we can also refer to Pascual's statements regarding his painting, equally applicable to his poems. The transformative power of the work affects not only the creator but also the person who sees a painting or reads a poem:

> As a reflection of that process of internal alchemy... the finished picture will have accomplished its purpose for the artist, but according to its perfection, the work will, like an echo, arouse a memory of the archetypes in the receptive viewer.... The viewer will benefit in function of the spiritual depth of the work and his own contemplativity....[10]

What is the meaning for the artist or poet of 'that process of internal alchemy'? It is an inner transformation that goes beyond self-observation in the sense that it is an active process, a purification and a transcending of the exterior ego, which is subject to both self-delusion and the delusions of the world. The first step is to observe dispassionately one's own faults and limitations, one's own forgetting. For this to have permanence, there is the need for active

---

[9] See below 'DE LA BIENAMADA: ¡Ay, si allí fuera aceptado!... El universo en nosotros;/y nosotros, una gota de rocío.'

[10] *Nómadas* exhibition catalogue. Vicente Pascual interviewed by Agustín López Tobajas, 'Conversación con Vicente Pascual' reprinted in *Vicente Pascual 1989/2008: Opusculum*, 69–79.

vigilance, for finally the poet is concerned that the end result of the process of inner alchemy leads to self-knowledge.

The essence and final purpose of spiritual practice: dying to the things of this world and of the ego—he prays will lead to the path of return. In another writing he speaks of 'el camino de retorno del exilio' (the path of return from exile), the wandering pilgrim who has been exiled from his true home in the world of archetypes and must now seek a way to return.

These thoughts have resonance with the Buddhist idea of liberation from suffering, from the endless round of birth and death in this world, but in fact they are central to the spiritual path found in Christianity and many other traditions. For the poet and painter his craft is the means through which he may find the path of return: 'Art, all art, is above all a means to know ourselves and to realize in the heart what we have fleetingly intuited, or have mentally discerned, of that place from which we were exiled.'[11]

The present volume brings together selections from Pascual's three published books in Spanish, *A la vida*, *De la nada*, and *100 Vistas*, as well as selections from previously unpublished works: *Romancillos*, and other unpublished poems.

I was indeed fortunate to begin work on these translations with Vicente Pascual in 2006, two years before his passing. His clarifications of meanings, words and phrases in his poems were, not surprisingly, invaluable. Further invaluable aid has come later from his widow Ana Marquina, his daughter Cira Pascual-Marquina, Francesc Gutiérrez, Hernán and Leslie Cadavid, and James Gavin.

Without the help and dedication of co-translator Susana Marín, this volume would not have been possible. Susana not only caught obvious and not so obvious errors in the translating, but also has solved knotty problems with idioms and unusual word usages.

This introduction is drawn in part from my essay in Spiritus: A Journal of Christian Spirituality (vol. 15, no. 1, Spring 2015), '"In That Luminous Darkness": The Poetry of Vicente Pascual Rodrigo.' My thanks go to Poetry Editor Mark Burrows and Editor Douglas

---

[11] Ibid., 75.

Christie for encouraging me to write and submit the essay and for their helpful suggestions.

Finally, we would like to thank Juan Acevedo and The Matheson Trust for their willingness to publish Vicente Pascual poetry and thus making his work more accessible to English-speaking readers.

William Wroth

A NOTE ON THE TRANSLATIONS

William Wroth started working on the translations in this volume in collaboration with Vicente Pascual in the last few years of Vicente's life. In December 2018, as William was diagnosed with a terminal illness, he tasked himself with completing the translation of all of Vicente's poems. When he asked me to assist him, I agreed with pleasure as I was struck by the richness of meaning and the beautiful usage of the Spanish language in Vicente's poetry.

In February 2019, I visited William and his wife Deborah in Santa Fe, New Mexico. In their adobe house overlooking the mountains we worked on Vicente's poems every day, enjoying our dicussions of words, meanings, and turns of expressions, often marvelling at the depth of spiritual realities that these poems evoke. It was also at that time that the Matheson Trust agreed to publish a selection of Vicente's poems. This was a project very dear to William's heart and I am glad that he was able to fulfil his wish of having Vicente Pascual's poetry published in bilingual edition for the benefit of English-speaking readers before his own passing on November 10, 2019.

Susana Marín

A LA VIDA

TO LIFE

DE LA VIDA

¡Venid,
guerreros, amantes y letrados!
Calentaos en mi hoguera,
que hace frío en esta noche
y quizás no haya mañana.

OF LIFE

Come,
warriors, lovers and wise men!
Warm yourselves around my fire,
it's cold tonight
and there may be no tomorrow.

DE LA MUERTE

Como esa noche tan clara
que sólo es de luz ausencia.
Ay, cautiva noche oscura,
¿de qué velo eres carencia?

OF DEATH

Like that night so clear
which is only absence of light.
O captive dark night,
which veil are you missing?

DE LA BIENAMADA

Me dijo la bella joven
que el carácter del silencio
queda lejos de afonía.
Que está vivo, siempre vivo.

Y el silencio cómo ruge,
con rugido silencioso.

OF THE BELOVED

The beautiful girl told me
that the nature of silence
is far from voicelessness.
That it is alive, always alive.

And silence, how it roars,
with a silent roaring.

DE LA VIDA

Cierro aquí y ahora estos ojos
en la cueva murmurando.
Siento la brisa de oriente
bajo el frondoso ciruelo.

Cierro aquí y ahora los ojos,
bajo el árbol murmurando.
Y hay aromas que me envuelven,
sobre esta noble montaña.

Cierro esos ojos, ahora,
en el monte, murmurando.
Brisa y aromas ya no siento.
Es sólo él quien me susurra.

OF LIFE

Here and now I close these eyes
murmuring in the grotto.
I feel the eastern breeze
underneath the leafy plum.

Here and now I close my eyes
murmuring under the tree.
And on this noble mountain
fragrances envelop me.

I close those eyes now,
murmuring on the mountain.
Breeze and fragrances I no longer feel.
It is only he who whispers to me.

DE LA BIENAMADA

¿Ves, amada?
¿Ves las nubes cómo bajan?
Cómo visten aquel monte.

¿Ves su cima, que se eleva,
que se asienta sobre ellas?
¿Ves mi pecho dilatado?

¿Ves, amada, lo que ves?
Es el cielo en nuestra tierra
y la tierra en nuestro cielo.

OF THE BELOVED

Do you see, Beloved?
Do you see how the clouds descend?
How they clothe that mountain.

Do you see its soaring peak,
standing above them?
Do you see my expanded breast?

Do you see, Beloved, what you see?
It is heaven on our earth
and earth in our heaven.

DE LA VIDA

Id por el mundo soñando
y si os parece triunfando
que yo aquí duermo ignorando.

OF LIFE

Go dreaming through the world
and if you like, be triumphant,
for I sleep here, unconcerned.

DE LA MUERTE

Cuando yo fui alumbrado
ya conmigo tú naciste.
¡Oh, mi muerte!

Esperando ese instante
en queriendo hurtar mi vida,
esperando ser en ella.

Cuánto querría yo ser
una muy leve humedad.
Que creciera en grandes nubes,
que muriera siendo lluvia.

Y entre vidas un descanso
dando vida, dando vida.

Y es que a mí se me parece
que con muerte viene vida.
¡Oh, mi muerte!

OF DEATH

When I first came into the light
you were already born with me
O my death!

Waiting for that instant
wanting to steal my life,
waiting to be part of it.

How I would like to be
a very faint moisture.
That would grow into great clouds,
that would die becoming rain.

And between lives a repose
giving life, giving life.

For it seems to me
that with death comes life.
O my death!

DE LA VIDA

Ay, me acuerdo, anciano 'Isa.
La mañana en que te fuiste,
tu figura noble y áurea.
Bien recuerdo, amigo 'Isa.

Ay, recuerdo, antiguo amigo
esa calma del recuerdo.
Y el aroma de tu muerte.

Bien me acuerdo, buen maestro,
echar tierra en aquel bosque,
en la fosa, en esa cueva.

Dejaste aquí un viejo cuerpo
y un poquico de aquel ser
que sólo era conocer.

Cómo añoro aquel momento
de ese ensueño en mi sueño.
Cuando entonces tu latido
y el latido que era mío
fueron sólo un solo aliento.

No te fuiste, viejo amigo,
que buen vino nos dejaste.

OF LIFE

I remember, revered 'Isa.
The morning you went away,
your noble, golden form.
Well I remember, friend 'Isa.

O I remember, old friend,
that peace of the remembrance.
And the fragrance of your death.

Well I remember, good master,
in those woods, throwing earth
into the grave, into that cave.

You left behind an aged body
and a little part of your being
that was pure knowing.

How I miss that moment,
that dream within my dream.
That moment when your heartbeat
and mine
became but a single breath.

You have not gone away, old friend,
for you have left us with good wine.

DE LA BIENAMADA

Como ese árbol
que en el páramo da fresco.

Como ese claro
que a la luz abre camino,
en un bosque muy sombrío.

Así es mi bienamada:
amor, dicha y reposo.

OF THE BELOVED

Like that tree
which gives coolness in the desert.

Like that clearing
which in a very dark wood
opens the way to light.

Such is my beloved:
love, joy and repose.

DE LA MUERTE

Ay, de quién, yo me pregunto.
¿De quién son estos mis versos?
¿De quién son si es que son ciertos?
Siendo entonces sólo un eco.

OF DEATH

O, whose verses, I ask myself,
whose are these verses of mine?
Whose are they, if they are true?
For my verses are only an echo.

DE LA BIENAMADA

¡Ay, si allí fuera aceptado!
Y mi alma reposara
en el pecho del amado.

Bienamada, ¿estás despierta?

Allí tu alma y mi espíritu,
y tu espíritu y mi alma,
sólo son respiro eterno.

El universo en nosotros;
y nosotros, una gota de rocío.

OF THE BELOVED

O if I were welcomed there!
And my soul were to repose
in the breast of the Beloved!

Dear Heart, are you awake?

There your soul and my spirit,
and your spirit and my soul,
they are only eternal breath.

The universe within us;
and we a drop of dew.

DE LA MUERTE

Está la emoción quebrada,
bajan lágrimas quemando.
Y este cuerpo, dolorido.

No ha de andar lejos la muerte,
que yo sin quererlo río,
o cuando menos sonrío,
viendo un perro o un gatico.

Ojalá quede cordura
cuando llegue ese momento,
el momento del encuentro.

¡Qué terrible y apacible está la mar!
Tan salada y tan lejana.

OF DEATH

The heart is broken,
Burning tears are falling.
And this body, so afflicted.

Death must not be far away,
without wanting to I laugh,
or at least I am smiling,
seeing a dog or an alley cat.

May some sanity be left
when that moment comes,
the moment when we meet.

How terrible, how peaceful is the sea!
So salty and so far away.

DE LA MUERTE

En la vida nada encuentro
y en la muerte todo añoro.

Mas no hay vida si ésta ignora
que es en muerte donde vive,
que es en ella que culmina.

Es por ello que deseo
el vivir mi propia muerte
con los ojos bien abiertos.

Y es que la vida y la muerte,
y también mi bienamada,
son lo mismo, eso creo.

OF DEATH

In life I find nothing
and in death I long for everything.

But there's no life if life knows not
that it lives in death,
that in death it culminates.

For this reason I desire
to live my own death
with eyes wide open.

For life and death
and also my beloved
are all the same, this I believe.

DE LA VIDA

Pero había un viejo anciano
que, ignorando, era muy sabio,
al que algunos tanteaban:

Has vivido muchos años,
has vivido en muchos tiempos.
Dinos tú, tan pobre sabio,
si aún deseo en ti algo queda.

Sí, aquí está, allí lo tengo.
No desear sólo deseo.

OF LIFE

There once was a venerable old man
who, in unknowing, was very wise,
and some tried to test him:

You have lived many years,
you have lived in many eras.
Tell us, poor wise man,
if a little bit of desire is still left in you.

Yes, here it is, there I have it.
Not to desire is my sole desire.

DE LA BIENAMADA

Y estas piedras.
¿Cuánto amor gastaron ya?
En queriendo ser guijarros.

OF THE BELOVED

And these stones.
How much love did they already waste?
In wanting to be pebbles.

DE LA BIENAMADA

Es un velo y un desvelo,
dulce velo transparente.

Ese velo que me atrapa,
me adormece y me somete.
Ese velo que me eleva,
me adormece y me somete.

Y es así ¿o me equivoco?
Que hay dos velos y dos hombres
en un velo y en un hombre.

¡Ayudadme, me emborracho!
¿O es que muero en mi desvelo?

OF THE BELOVED

It is a veil and an unveiling,
sweet transparent veil.

That veil which traps me,
lulls me to sleep and subdues me.
That veil which exalts me,
lulls me to sleep and subdues me.

And that's how it is, or am I mistaken?
That there are two veils and two men
in one veil and in one man.

Help me, I am getting drunk!
Or am I dying in my unveiling?

DE LA MUERTE

Que mis huesos se evaporen
en el aire muy inmenso.
Que mis carnes alimenten
muy menudas criaturas.

Y ojalá que este romero
en muriendo siempre, encuentre
el sendero de retorno.

OF DEATH

May my bones vanish
in the immensity of air.
May my flesh be food
for the smallest creatures.

And may this pilgrim
by always dying, find
the path of return.

DE LA MUERTE

Y cuando venga la muerte
me dirá: *ya está.*
Le diré: *¿ya está?*
Y me dirá: *ya está.*

OF DEATH

And when death comes
she will say to me: *this is it.*
I will say to her: *this is it?*
And she will say to me: *this is it.*

DE LA NADA

FROM NOTHING

ABRÍOS

Abríos, vosotros los cielos.
Rasgad, truenos, la afonía.
Horadad, rayos, la umbría.

Que acaezcan grandes aguas.
Y que alguna me dé alcance
y con ella la entereza,
de vivir mi propia muerte.

OPEN UP

Open up, O you heavens.
Break the silence, thunderclaps.
Pierce the shadows, lightning bolts.

May great torrents burst forth.
And may one overtake me
and bring with it the courage
to live my own death.

AFUERA

Afuera, iros afuera,
contemplando lo que hay dentro.

Tomad sus caballos,
mellad sus espadas.
Que ya no disciernen.

Reíd de su espanto,
llorad su locura
sufriendo la escarcha,
sufriendo los rayos.

Miraos en ellos
y ved lo que somos.

GO OUT

Out, go out,
to contemplate what is within.

Take their horses,
notch their swords.
For they no longer discern.

Laugh at their fear,
cry at their folly
suffering frosts,
suffering heat.

See yourselves in them
and see what we are.

COMO AQUEL

Como aquel pájaro herido
se refugia entre los bosques.
Así anduvo el buen anciano.

Engañado por el mundo.

Y sufriendo un sol de espanto.
En buscando la frescura,
muy cansado miró al cielo,
fatigado, al corazón.

Fue allí que él se ocultó.
Con su voz, dicen, se fue.

LIKE THAT

Like that wounded bird
taking shelter in the woods.
Thus the good old man made his way.

Deceived by the world.

And suffering the blazing sun.
Searching for coolness,
very weary he looked to the heavens,
exhausted he looked to the heart.

That was where he hid himself.
With his voice, they say, he was gone.

EL MUNDO

El mundo era oscuro,
nocturna la cueva.
Ni aroma, ni ruido.

Nada distingo, todo es sólo uno.

THE WORLD

The world was dark,
as the cave at night.
No fragrance, no noise.

I see nothing, everything is one.

DIME TÚ

Dime tú, anciana muerte.
¿Eres alba?, ¿eres ocaso?
Y la muerte va y me dice:
Eres tú quien lo decide.

Me puse a reír,
me puse a temblar.

TELL ME

Tell me, venerable death.
Are you dawn? Are you sundown?
And death comes and says to me:
You are the one to decide.

I began to laugh,
I began to tremble.

EL SUFRIR

El sufrir de tantos seres,
encuentra el eco en mi llanto.
¿Por qué te escondes, bienamada?

Dime tú, mi buen romero,
¿a mi amiga has tu avistado?
¿Tiene en su cantar luceros?

SUFFERING

The suffering of so many beings
finds an echo in my weeping.
Why are you hiding, beloved?

Tell me my good pilgrim,
Have you seen my friend?
Does she have stars shining in her song?

MAÑANA

Mañana, quizás, Dios sabe,
testifique un gran milagro.
Mi corazón aún latiendo
y tus ojos en los míos.

Y los chopos, que ya brotan.

TOMORROW

Tomorrow, perhaps, God knows,
I may witness a great miracle.
My heart still beating
and your eyes in mine.

And the poplars, now budding.

ESTAD ATENTOS

Estad atentos.
A la muerte.
Dice *voy*, y no ha venido.
Iré más tarde, y ya ha cumplido.

PAY ATTENTION

Pay attention.
To death.
It says, *I'm coming*, and has not come.
I will come later, and has already come.

MAS ME ACUERDO

Mas me acuerdo de esa noche
que volvime a aquel mi origen.
Siete vueltas di danzando.
A mi izquierda el eje santo.
Era negro y yo vacío.

Pero olvido llega pronto,
al espanto del barranco.

Sólo en ti hallo refugio,
aquí adentro y en lo alto.

HOW WELL I REMEMBER

How well I remember that night
when I returned to my origin.
Seven times I danced around.
To my left the sacred center.
It was black and I was empty.

But soon I became forgetful,
in fear of the precipice.

Only in thee do I find refuge,
here within and above.

ME QUEMAN

Me queman los párpados,
mejillas y sienes.
Esas lágrimas ardientes,
y ese pecho comprimido.

Tanto ego, tanto ruido,
tanto infierno, tanto limbo.

Y esa luz entre las cañas.
¿Quién la mira? ¿quién la mira?

MY EYELIDS

My eyelids, cheeks and temples
are burning.
Those fiery tears
and that anguished breast.

So much ego, so much noise,
so much hell, so much limbo.

And that light among the reeds
Who sees it, who sees it?

MIRAD

¡Mirad, viene la lluvia, mirad!

Trae la vida, trae la vida.
¡Qué vergüenza, de mis llantos!
En la noche, siempre clara.

Qué bien juntos andan siempre
la memoria y el olvido.

LOOK

Look, here comes the rain, look!

It brings life, it brings life.
How shameful is my weeping!
In the night, ever clear.

How closely together they always go,
remembrance and forgetfulness.

NO OIGO

No oigo el eco de su canto.
Miro al río y viene un trueno.
Yo me escondo, me da miedo,
el mirarle frente a frente.

I CANNOT HEAR

I cannot hear the echo of his song.
I look at the river and thunder comes.
I hide myself, it frightens me,
seeing him face to face.

OJALÁ

Ojalá estuviera siempre
tu dulce nombre trovando.
Y el aliento sostenido.

Mantenme siempre en tu canto.
Mi corazón viendo y estando,
por tu saber temblando,
se esconde en tu nombre admirado.
No dejes que yo te olvide.

Mantenme siempre en tu canto.

Que es muy áspera y muy pobre
esta tierra que me diste.

I WISH I WERE ALWAYS

I wish I were always
singing your sweet name.
With steady breath.

Keep me always in your song.
My heart seeing and being,
and trembling in your wisdom,
is hidden in your honoured name.
Don't allow me to forget you.

Keep me always in your song.

For very harsh and poor
is this world that you have given me.

PASARÁN

Pasarán aquellas dichas
así como los pesares.

Nada queda, no hay ni huella,
de los giros de las aves.
De sus cantos, cuando emigran.

THOSE JOYS WILL PASS

Those joys will pass
as well as the sorrows.

Nothing is left, there is not even a trace,
of the darting birds.
Of their songs, when they fly away.

QUÉ MEJOR

¿Qué mejor puedo añorar,
que dejar, siendo, de ser?
En los bosques y en las vegas,
con las aves y el silencio.

El dolor y tantas penas,
el rigor y la dulzura.
La certeza de unos pasos
que me llevan hacia dentro.

¡Mirad, están danzando!

WHAT BETTER

What better can I yearn for
than to let go of life while living?
In the woods and in the meadows
with the birds and the silence.

Sorrow and so much pain,
rigor and gentleness.
The certitude of steps
that are leading me inward.

Look, they are dancing!

TIENE NEGRAS

Tiene muy negras pupilas
y adormece mi mirada.

¿Donde vive el gran silencio?
En las tierras más comunes.
Junto al agua, y lejos de ella.

En sus labios temblorosos.

SHE HAS BLACK

She has very black eyes
and she calms my gaze.

Where does the great silence dwell?
In the most ordinary places.
Near the water, and far from it.

In her trembling lips.

QUISIERA

Quisiera ser no querer.
O mejor, ser siendo en ti.

Sufrir, gozar, existir.
Dar, morir en el amar.
Pensar, ver y recordar,
confiando.

Aterido y tembloroso,
sudoroso, estoy soñando.

Y hay presencia en la ausencia,
si es de noche.

I WISH

I wish to live without wanting.
Or better yet, to live in thee.

To suffer, to delight, to exist.
To give, to die in love.
To think, to see, to remember,
with trust.

Shivering and trembling,
sweating, I dream.

And there is presence in absence,
when it is night.

QUE MORIR

Que morir está en vivir,
el vivir no es sino amar.
Y que amar es un morir
y morir es conocer.

Que es por eso que me acuerdo.

DYING

For dying is in living,
living is only to love.
And to love is to die
and to die is to know.

That is why I remember.

Y OCURRIÓ

Y ocurrió lo que no ocurre,
el ahora nunca muere.
El presente que fue entonces,
un futuro y un jamás.

En la muerte es que coincide
lo que dura por un tiempo
y lo Eterno, que no muda.

Misterioso es este istmo.

Rezo y rezo en el silencio.
Callo y callo, mientras canto.

AND IT HAPPENED

And what doesn't happen, happened,
the now never dies.
The present that was then,
a future and a never.

In death what endures for a time
converges with the Eternal,
which is immutable.

Mysterious is this junction.

I pray and pray in silence.
I keep quiet, quiet while I sing.

Y AUNQE

Y aunque sé eso que sé,
que naciendo yo nací,
que muriendo moriré.

Es naciendo que morí
y muriendo que nací.

AND EVEN THOUGH

And even though I know what I know,
that being born I was born,
and dying I will die.

In being born I died
and in dying I was born.

Y QUITÉ

Y quité aquellas nubes
que cubrían esos montes.

Y aparté aquellas nieves
que alegraban muchas piedras.

Vi otra forma que nacía,
otra forma del silencio.

Arranqué rocas y riscos.

Y óyeme, mi buen amigo:
al quitar lo que era monte
sólo cueva me quedó,
que era adentro, como afuera.

I TOOK AWAY

And I took away those clouds
that covered up the mountains.

And I removed those snows
that brightened so many stones.

I saw the birthing of another form,
another form of silence.

I uprooted rocks and crags.

And listen, my good friend:
Taking away what was mountain
left me only with the cave,
which was the same within as without.

EN TU AUSENCIA

En tu ausencia
nada encuentro.
Ni aun siquiera la nostalgia,
ni aun siquiera larga espera.

Mas me han dicho lo que dicen,
lo que dicen los que saben,
que el ausente te conoce,
que te ama y que te siente.

Y los sauces cómo danzan,
cuando el cierzo los encuentra.

IN YOUR ABSENCE

In your absence
I find nothing.
Not even longing,
not even expectation.

But they have said to me what they say,
what they say, those who know,
is that the absent one knows you,
he loves and feels for you.

And the willows how they dance,
when the north wind finds them.

Y CUANDO

Y cuando al fin me pregunten,
diré soy sólo él.

Eso espera el pordiosero.
Como el sol y el leve junco.

AND WHEN

And when at the end they would ask me,
I will say I am only He.

That is what the beggar waits for.
Like the sun and the delicate reed.

100 VISTAS

~

100 VIEWS

¡Qué vértigo
tanto esfuerzo para un náufrago!
sobre el abismo
y enamorado de la luna.

∿

Llueve mucho, llueve mucho.
¿Ves la tierra, la hueles?
Su oración humedece mis ojos.

What dizziness!
Such a struggle for a castaway!
On the edge of the abyss
And smitten by the moon.

~

So much rain, so much rain.
Do you see the earth, can you smell it?
Its prayer moistens my eyes.

Dicen que lo de allí
antes ya lo hemos gustado.
Pero no sé qué es antes o después,
pues aquí, como allí, todo es ahora.

∾

Pero dancemos
hacia el norte, hacia el sur,
al este y al oeste.
En el centro, recios,
dancemos en el centro.

They say we have tasted beforehand
what is to come hereafter.
But I do not know what is before or after,
because here, like there, everything is now.

∾

But let us dance
towards the north, towards the south,
to the east and to the west.
In the center: let us dance
with power in the center.

Cómo sonríen
los cipreses, los almendros,
el romero y el tomillo.
Hasta la tierra,
tan austera, sonríe.

~

Allí no hay ruidos, nada pasa.
Sólo se oye el silencio.
¡Elevad vuestras voces,
laúdes y armonios! ¡Cantad aquí
ese vuestro elocuente silencio!

How they smile
the cypresses, the almonds,
the rosemary and the thyme.
Even the earth,
so austere, is smiling.

≈

Over there, no noise, nothing happens.
One hears only silence.
Raise your voices,
lutes and harmoniums! Sing here
your eloquent silence!

POEMAS INÉDITOS

❧

UNPUBLISHED POEMS

~

ROMANCILLOS

BALLADS

~

AHORAM

Ahora me acuerdo, ahora recuerdo.
Dices, buen amigo, que es áspera la vida,
las flores y el amar.
Y qué sé yo si en cuanto miras,
aspereza sólo encuentras.

Pero dime, buen amigo:
¿qué sería?
¿si gemelo de su molde todo fuera?

¿Qué sería de nostalgia?
¡Qué sería de la noche?
cuando anhelas.

¿Qué sería de tu llanto,
y de tu hombría?

Qué bien se ve en esta cueva,
si bien se mira y está oscura.

AHORAM*

Now I remember, now I recall.
You say, good friend, that life is harsh,
as are the flowers and love.
And how would I know if, as soon as you look,
you only find harshness.

But tell me, good friend:
what would it be?
if everything were a true cast of its mold?

What would longing be?
What would become of the night?
when you are yearning.

What would become of your tears,
and of your valour?

How well one sees in this cave,
if one looks deeply and it is dark.

* T.N.– Original titles, not translated. The author made up the titles of
'Romancillos' by combining the first word of the poem with some
letters of the second and sometimes the third words.

ALLIES

Allí, eso creo, había un viejo,
que reía, que reía,
y que a veces era serio.

Y decía, y decía:
no busques sabiduría.
Te eludirá si la buscas,
te buscará si la ignoras.

Sólo una cosa más decía serio,
más que serio, el grave anciano:
teme, sabiendo lo que temes,
distingue entre opinión y certeza.

ALLIES

There, I believe, was an old man,
who laughed and laughed,
and who at times was serious.

And he said, and he said:
don't look for wisdom.
It will elude you if you look for it,
it will look for you if you ignore it.

Only one more thing,
said the grave old one, more than earnest:
be afraid, knowing what you fear,
distinguish between opinion and certitude.

ENLOA

En lo alto del mundo yo estaba,
aceptando tu tierna mirada.
Fue entonces que yo contemplé
en tus ojos la noche profunda.

En noche callada soñé
que acudía contigo danzando
por los valles que nacen de ti
respirando la dulce palabra.

Junto al lecho en que yo reposaba
mis amigos tomaron mi mano
comprendieron que yo ya me fui.
Que allí aguardo, muy borracho.

ENLOA

I stood at the top of the world
receiving your tender gaze.
It was then that I contemplated
in your eyes the profound night.

In the silent night I dreamt
I came dancing with you
through valleys born from you
breathing the sweet word.

Next to the bed in which I was resting
my friends took my hand
they knew that I had already gone away.
For there I wait, very drunk.

NUNCAD

Nunca dudes, bienamada,
del amor que en mí hay por ti.

Nunca dudes, bienamada,
del amor de Dios
que por ti hay en mí.

Nunca dudes, bienamada,
del amor de Dios
que por ti hay en ti.

NUNCAD

Never doubt, Beloved,
the love there is for thee in me.

Never doubt, Beloved,
the love of God
there is for thee in me.

Never doubt, Beloved,
the love of God
there is for thee in thee.

PEROE

Pero el mundo ya era otro.
Yo era un niño y ya sabía,
ya sabía quién pasaba.
Me hincaron de rodillas
y miraba el ancho río.

De arco en arco,
de arco en arco por el puente.
Padre Nuestro, Ave María.
Y dar vida, dando vida.

Hace poco, bien recuerdo,
se me vino él a mi sueño.
¡Qué joven que eres, padre!
¡Hay que ver qué joven eres!

¡Y qué es un río, si no hay agua!
¿Y qué es del agua si no hay cauce?

PEROE

But now the world had changed.
I was a child and I knew,
already knew who was passing on.
They made me kneel down
and I looked out at the wide river.

From arch to arch,
from arch to arch along the bridge.
Padre Nuestro, Ave María.
Giving life, giving life.

Recently, I remember well,
in my dream he came to me.
How young you are, Father!
O how young you are!

And what is a river, if there is no water!
And what about water, if there's no riverbed?

SIENC

Si encuentras dormido
a mi corazón,
dejalo, no lo despiertes,
que lo real es su sueño.
Y también lo es el buen vino.

SIENC

If you find
my heart asleep,
leave it alone, don't wake it up,
for what is real is its dream.
And it is also the good wine.

YCRUZAN

Y cruzando aquellas aguas
del torrente traicionero.
He buscado quien me guíe,
he buscado quien me guíe.

Sólo alguno que no siendo,
por no siendo, siempre fuera.
¿Cómo sabes el camino,
ay mendigo venerable?

Nunca olvides, buen amigo,
que es muy poco lo que sabes.
Ay mendigo, ay pordiosero.

YCRUZAN

And crossing the treacherous torrent
of those waters.
I have looked for someone to guide me,
I have looked for someone to guide me.

Only someone who, not being,
by not being, always was.
How do you know the way,
oh venerable mendicant?

Never forget, good friend,
how very little you know.
Oh mendicant, oh beggar.

YUNIVER

Y, universo, óyeme.
Qué tú y yo todo siendo,
nada somos.

YUNIVER

And, Universe, hear me.
That you and I, being everything,
are nothing.

OTROS POEMAS

~

OTHER POEMS

~

AQUÍ HUBO

Aquí hubo vida alguna vez.
Osamentas y vestigios.
Y no sabe que es la vida,
ni grandeza, ni belleza,
quien la muerte no recuerda.

~

ES MUY

Es muy temprano
y el agua está fría.
¿Oís mis latidos?
Pues ni aun ellos, ni aun ellos,
ni aun ellos son míos.

HERE WAS

Here there once was life.
Bones and vestiges.
And he does not know what life is
neither grandeur nor beauty,
he who does not remember death.

≈

IT IS VERY

It is very early
and the water is cold.
Do you hear my heartbeats?
Well not even they, not even they,
not even they are mine.

HEMOS

Hemos estado con unos
que en ti rememoraban.

– ¿Estaban ellos muy atentos?
– Sólo en ti se refugiaban.
– ¿Sabían ésos lo que hacían?
– Sabrían, pues se entregaban.
– Decidme si ellos algo pedían.
– Tu nombre les compensaba.
– ¿Es que acaso eran muy blandos?
– Su confianza les quemaba.
– Y del mundo ¿qué decían?
– Que por sí mismo nada era.
– Y pues siendo ¿qué es lo que era?
– Que el mundo y ellos en ti eran.
– Que vengan, aquí espero

WE HAVE

We have been with those
who remembered Thee.

– Were they very attentive?
– Only in thee they sought refuge.
– Did they know what they were doing?
– They must have known, because they were so devoted
– Tell me if they asked for something.
– Thy name was recompense enough.
– By chance were they too weak?
– They were kindled by their trust.
– And what did they say about the world?
– That in itself it was nothing.
– And that being so, then what was it?
– That both they and the world were in thee.
– Then let them come, here I wait.

ME ACERCO

Me acerco a la tapia y oigo las flores,
escucho cipreses, castaños y almendros.

Dime, viejo, buen guardián.
¿Cómo entrar en tanta dicha?
y llorar en armonía.
¿El sentir la dulce lluvia?
La embriaguez, del muy buen vino.

Tu mirada y tu silencio,
buen guardián, me aterrorizan.

¿En mi llanto y en mi risa?
¿En mis venas que son tuyas?

¡Qué fresco se está aquí adentro!

I COME NEAR

I come near the wall and hear the flowers,
I listen to the cypresses, the chestnut and the almond trees.

Tell me, old man, good guardian,
how to come to such bliss?
And in harmony, to weep.
Feeling the sweet rain?
The intoxication, of very good wine.

Your gaze and your silence,
Good guardian, frighten me.

In my tears and in my laughter?
In my veins that belong to you?

What coolness is here inside!

INDEX OF FIRST LINES

www.ingramcontent.com/pod-product-compliance
Lightning Source LLC
Chambersburg PA
CBHW032003040426
42448CB00006B/475

* 9 7 8 1 9 0 8 0 9 2 1 9 9 *